NATIONAL FOOTBALL LEAGUE
BEHIND THE SCENES

by Joe Layden

SCHOLASTIC INC.

New York   Toronto   London   Auckland   Sydney
Mexico City   New Delhi   Hong Kong   Buenos Aires

January 26, 2003

It is one of the most breathtaking moments in all of sports.

This is after the National Anthem has been played. After the fighter jets have roared overhead and the pregame introductions have been completed. As the afternoon sun slides toward the horizon, two teams take the field for the final National Football League game of the season, a game known simply and elegantly as the Super Bowl. At one end of San Diego's Qualcomm Stadium are the Tampa Bay Buccaneers, champions of the National Football Conference. Fanning out across the other end are the AFC champion Oakland Raiders.

THIS GAME, THIS MOMENT, IS THE CULMINATION OF SO MUCH WORK, SO MUCH EFFORT.

As the ball is teed up, the stadium becomes eerily quiet. It's as if 70,000 people are holding their breath, all at the same time. You can almost hear the players' hearts beating, imagine what is going through their minds. This game, this moment, is the culmination of so much work, so much effort. Five months earlier there were 32 teams and almost two thousand athletes who clung to the belief that they could win this game. But now there are only two. Soon there will be only one.

As the referee presses a whistle against his lips, the kicker raises a single fist—a signal to all that the game is about to begin. Suddenly the crowd exhales. There is a collective buzz in the air, a hum that intensifies as the kicker drops his arm and begins to move toward the ball. He takes three quick steps—one-two-three! —and swings his leg sharply. The ball explodes off the tee and sails end over end across a brilliant blue California sky. In a matter of seconds, the field will be alive with the sound of men grunting and yelling, of pads smacking against pads. They won't hear it in the stadium, of course, where the wild cheering of fans drowns out everything else. Neither will it be heard by the tens of millions of fans watching on television at home. To them, the game is a spectacle, a beautiful and graceful ballet performed by men with uncommon agility and strength. On the field, though, it is also a game of courage and determination— even here, at its highest level, on the most important day of the season.

That much hasn't changed.

It's hard sometimes to think of the NFL as anything but a distant relative of the game that was invented so many years ago. This is especially true on Super Bowl Sunday, a day so big that it has become an unoffi-

SIMEON RICE OF THE TAMPA BAY BUCCANEERS, 2001.

4

cial holiday in American culture. People plan huge parties around Super Bowl Sunday. Newspapers devote pages of coverage to the game. Advertisers save their best and most interesting television commercials for Super Bowl Sunday, because they know the audience will be one of the biggest of the year. It seems as though everyone watches the Super Bowl, even people who aren't really football fans. All of which makes the game seem bigger than life.

That's not quite true, of course, but there's no denying that football in the twenty-first century is a whole lot bigger than it was in 1869, when Rutgers and Princeton played the very first college football game. Actually, the game they played was more like a combination of football, soccer, and rugby, but on that day the seeds of popularity were planted.

Thanks in no small part to a man named Walter Camp, football gained widespread acceptance in the late nineteenth century. Camp played an early version of football when he was a student at Yale University. He later became the team's coach and helped adopt a set of rules to govern the new sport. It was Camp who came up with the idea of separating each team's possession into a set of "downs." He also devised football's first numerical scoring system (two points for a safety, two points for an extra point, four points for a touchdown, and five points for a field goal). For his contributions, Camp is often credited with being the "father" of the sport of football. But you have to wonder if he would recognize his "child" today.

As any fan knows, professional football is not only a game, but a very competitive business. Only a handful of men have the talent and ambition to make it in the NFL, and they're paid very well for their work. That wasn't the case in 1920, when the league was born. Back then, professional football players didn't make much money. They all had jobs and careers outside of football. Many of them, in fact, worked second jobs during the season!

Not that they cared. Professional football players in the early days of the NFL considered themselves fortunate to get paid for playing a game they loved. And they did love it, despite the fact that it was a challenging sport. There was no specialization in

HAROLD "RED" GRANGE OF THE CHICAGO BEARS, 1925.

the 1920s. Just about everyone played two positions: one on offense and one on defense. A running back, for example, usually played defensive back as well. Linemen just shifted from one side of the ball to the other. There was no rest for the weary.

Football has always been a tough sport. That's no surprise, really. If you look at photographs of the early NFL, you'll see players wearing thin leather sheaths that passed for helmets. (Some wore no helmets at all!) There were no face masks or mouthguards. They learned to take care of their equipment, because if something happened to it, the players were responsible for repairs. Sometimes they even sewed their own uniforms!

Conditions improved as the league expanded in the 1930s. Fans flocked to see the NFL's biggest stars, players with catchy names like Bronko Nagurski and "Red" Grange. But it wasn't until television brought the game into the homes of millions of Americans that the NFL really took flight. The first professional game

was broadcast in 1939, and by the 1950s football had become a staple of the American television diet. The 1958 NFL Championship Game between the New York Giants and the Baltimore Colts proved to be the perfect tease for anyone not yet familiar with pro football. In what is often called the greatest game ever played, the Colts beat the Giants, 23–17, in overtime to win the title.

Two years later the American Football League was formed as a rival to the established NFL. The champions of the two leagues played each other for the first time after the 1966 season. The game was billed as the "Super Bowl." No one had any idea then just how appropriate a name it would turn out to be. For there is no athletic event quite like the Super Bowl. It is, for many players, the defining moment of their careers. It is a game in which heroes are made. When we think of the greatest players in NFL history, we often think of their Super Bowl performances: Joe Namath in Super Bowl III, guiding the New York Jets to an upset of the Baltimore Colts; Joe Montana lead-

JOHNNY UNITAS OF
THE BALTIMORE COLTS,
1967.

6

ing the San Francisco 49ers to four Super Bowl titles in the 1980s; the Dallas Cowboys winning three Super Bowls in the 1990s behind quarterback Troy Aikman and running back Emmitt Smith; former Arena Football League quarterback Kurt Warner giving hope to minor leaguers everywhere by leading the 1999 St. Louis Rams to a championship.

For all of those players, and for anyone in the NFL today, football is far more than a hobby. It is a passion...a way of life. Success on the field comes at a price, and that price is hard work. A great coach once said, "Teams are made during the season, but players are made before the season." Ask anyone in the NFL, and they'll tell you that's the truth. The Vince Lombardi Trophy, awarded to the team that wins the Super Bowl, is the most cherished prize in football, maybe in all of sports. For a fortunate few, it's the pot of gold at the end of the rainbow, the final stop in a long, exhausting journey.

You might think that professional football players have it easy. You might think they have the greatest job in the world. If so, you're right...and you're wrong. It is a great job. Ask anyone in the NFL. But there's nothing easy about it. What you see on Sunday afternoon or Monday night is a precise performance honed and sharpened through endless hours on the practice field and in the weight room. If you want to know how Jerry Rice continues to shred defenses, even at the age of 40, all you have to do is follow him around in the offseason. Jerry trains every day, twelve months a year. He runs endless sprints and lifts weights until his muscles ache. Because he knows that preparation is the key to success. When training camp opens in July, and the real work begins, he's ready.

Summer is the harshest time for professional football players, a time when jobs are won and lost and careers are shaped. After holding "mini-camps" in the spring, each team conducts

GREEN BAY PACKERS QUARTERBACK BRETT FAVRE, 1998.

an intense summer training camp that spans several weeks. During this time the players eat, sleep, and breathe football. They often practice twice a day, sometimes under the glare of a blazing sun. When they aren't practicing, they're lifting weights, trying to get stronger, bigger, faster. Finally, when they're too tired to run another step or catch another pass, they move into the classroom. They study their playbooks, memorize offenses and defenses. They watch themselves on film and listen carefully as their coaches critique their strengths and weaknesses.

On and on it goes, until summer mercifully gives way to autumn, and the leaves begin to turn, and the smell of football fills the air. Training camp breaks. And not a moment too soon. The players are tired of the routine. They're eager to put on their uniforms and march into a stadium. They want to hear the exhilarating sound of 80,000 fans cheering as one. They're ready to play football!

The regular season, which stretches out over seventeen weeks, has a rhythm all its own. If you visit an NFL locker room on Monday morning, you'll find yourself surrounded by giant men walking with slow steps. They're completely exhausted after the weekend's game, and this is a day to recover and review what happened on Sunday. This is a part of the game that most fans never get a chance to see. Players wear armor and lift mountains of weights for a reason: to protect themselves. Football is a hard game, and no one goes through the season without a few bumps and bruises.

Tuesday is the players' day off, but the coaches work all day and into the night preparing the game plan for next week. On Wednesday, the players are back on the practice field. The next few days are a whirlwind of drills and meetings and film sessions. Each man has an assignment for the upcoming game, and he prepares for it just as a student might prepare for a test. The quarter-

JERRY RICE, WIDE RECEIVER FOR THE OAKLAND RAIDERS, 2002.

back, for example, throws dozens of passes against a defense similar to the one he will face on Sunday.

If a team is playing on the road, Friday or Saturday is a travel day. The players gather for a team meeting and a big meal Saturday night, and then sleep in their hotel rooms. They take a bus to the stadium early the next morning, arriving several hours before the fans. Each athlete prepares for the game in his own way. Some sit quietly at their lockers, reading or listening to music. Others pace nervously around the dressing room. Eventually they change into their uniforms. This can take some time. In fact, most players need assistance with their equipment. Helmets have to be adjusted, shoulder pads tightened. There are miles of tape to be unraveled.

Finally, it's game time. The players gather in the center of the room. The coach gives a pep talk. Sometimes a few of the players speak. They talk about bravery and teamwork. They promise to give their best, to leave nothing on the field. And then they march out of the locker room and through a tunnel beneath the stadium. The building shakes as they emerge from the darkness, out into

the light of a Sunday afternoon, or the lights of a Sunday or Monday night. By now the stadium is packed with fans who are ready for their weekly dose of football.

It's game time!

This is a scene that's played out across the country, week after week, in more than two dozen cities. The season rolls on. Stars emerge. Players who were unrecognizable in August become household names in November. Contenders separate themselves from the pack. That's the natural order of things. Not everyone can reach the playoffs. Only two teams make it to the Super Bowl.

Remember that the next time you watch football's biggest game. When you see the players take the field, think about how hard they've worked. Think about the hours and weeks and months of preparation. And remember...

They've earned it.

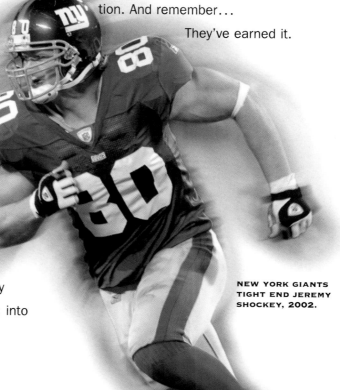

NEW YORK GIANTS
TIGHT END JEREMY
SHOCKEY, 2002.

THE EARLY YEARS

Legendary running back Jim Thorpe is one of the most recognizable names from pro football's infancy.

Jim Thorpe (left, reaching out with his left arm) playing for the Canton Bulldogs in a game against the Columbus Panhandles in 1915.

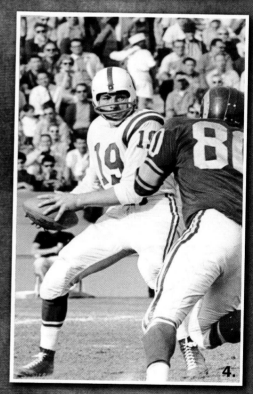

1. QB Sammy Baugh of the Washington Redskins, 1940. 2. Otto Graham runs against the Los Angeles Rams on Christmas Eve, 1950. 3. Bronko Nagurski of the Chicago Bears plows over a defender in the 1934 championship game vs. the New York Giants. 4. Hall of Fame quarterback Johnny Unitas of the Baltimore Colts on the move in a 1959 game. 5. Cycledrome, home of the Providence (Rhode Island) Steam Roller in the 1920s.

TRAINING CAMP

Veteran defensive lineman Michael Sinclair hits the pads on the opening day of the Denver Broncos training camp, 2002.

The Texas sun beats down on the Dallas Cowboys training camp, 1993.

1.

3.

1. New York Jets players get some fresh air and a preseason workout on the stationary bicycles, 1998. 2. Indianapolis Colts quarterback Peyton Manning takes the time to sign autographs on the first day of training camp, 1998. 3. Linebacker Tedy Bruschi hits the blocking sled at the New England Patriots training camp, 2002. 4. The San Francisco 49ers begin a long, full day of training with stretching exercises, 1998. 5. The 49ers work out on the big bag, 1998.

2.

4.

5.

EQUIPMENT

When an NFL team hits the road, they have to pack *everything*!

1.

2.

3.

4.

Football equipment has evolved and improved over the years, as seen in the ever-changing designs of the helmet. **1.** Jim Thorpe in the 1920s. **2.** Bill Dudley of the Detroit Lions, 1948. **3.** Alex Webster of the New York Giants, 1960. **4.** Joe Namath of the New York Jets, 1972. **5.** Julius Peppers of the Carolina Panthers, 2002

5.

Offensive Line Coach
Patrick Morris of the
San Francisco 49ers goes
over some plays in the
locker room at halftime,
1999.

1.

2.

3.

1. A St. Louis Rams lineman studies digital blocking photos taken from the coaches' upper level box during a game against Tampa Bay, 2002. 2. Jon Gruden calls out a play from the sideline, 2001. 3. Like many quarterbacks today, Chad Pennington of the New York Jets carries a set of plays on his left forearm, 2002. 4. Offensive line coach George Warhop of the Arizona Cardinals goes over blocking assignments during a game, 2001. 5. Special teams coach Brad Seely of the New England Patriots reviews a play diagram with team members at practice, 2002.

4.

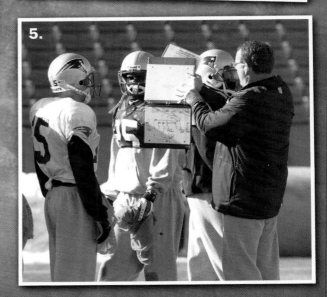

5.

THE COACHES

Baltimore Ravens coach Brian Billick receives a soaking to celebrate victory in Super Bowl XXXV.

Legendary coach of the Green Bay Packers Vince Lombardi after winning the 1966 NFL championship game.

1.

2.

3.

4

5.

1. Wide receiver Randy Moss and coach Dennis Green of the Minnesota Vikings. **2.** Miami Dolphins running back Ricky Williams speaking with a coach during a game, 2002. **3.** The unmistakable silhouette of Dallas Cowboys coaching great Tom Landry, in a 1988 game. **4.** The Arizona Cardinals coaching staff sport the latest in communications technology, 2000. **5.** Jets defensive coach, Rubin Carter, prepares the defensive linemen before a game, 2001. **6.** NFL Commissioner Pete Rozelle and Chicago Bears Head Coach Mike Ditka in New Orleans at Super Bowl XX, 1986.

6.

THE TRAINERS

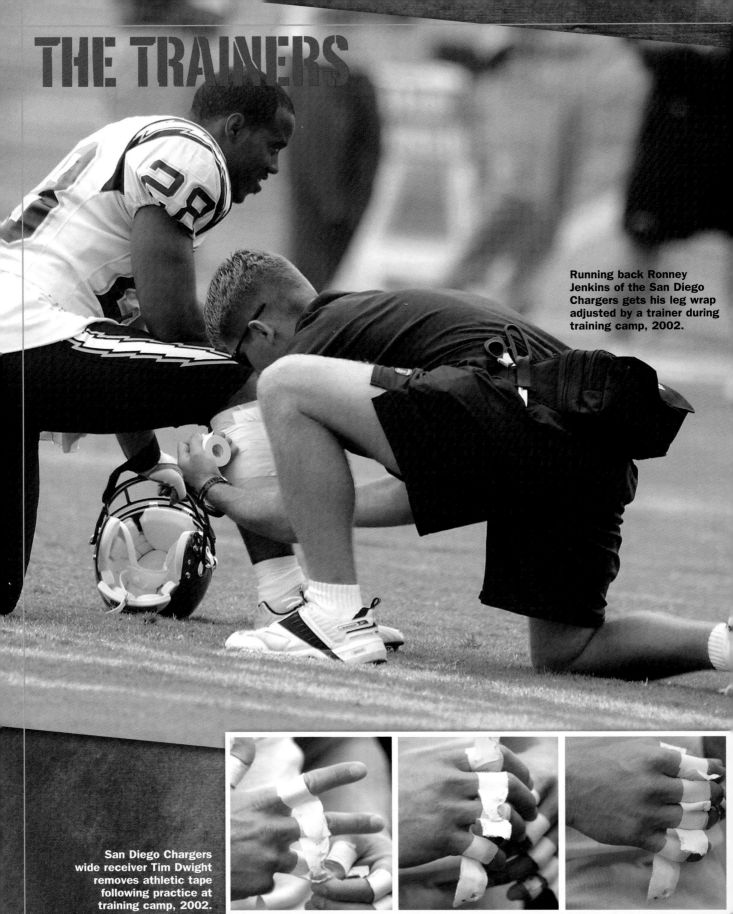

Running back Ronney Jenkins of the San Diego Chargers gets his leg wrap adjusted by a trainer during training camp, 2002.

San Diego Chargers wide receiver Tim Dwight removes athletic tape following practice at training camp, 2002.

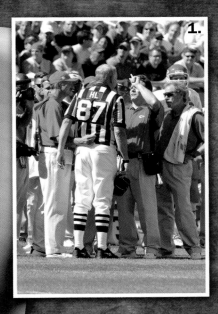

1.

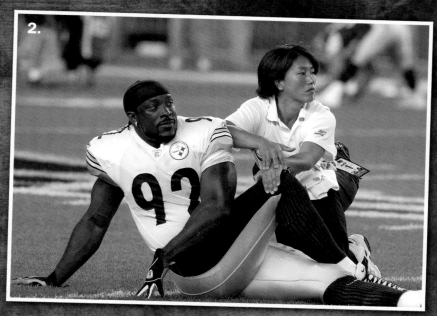

2.

3.

4.

1. Head lineman Paul Weidner is checked by the Kansas City Chiefs trainer after Weidner was injured during a game, 2002. **2.** Linebacker Jason Glidon of the Pittsburgh Steelers receives treatment from trainer Ariko Iso before a game in 2002. Iso is the first female trainer hired by an NFL team. **3.** A rolling Patriots trainer equipment box on the sideline during a game, 2001. **4.** A Miami Dolphins trainer stretching wide receiver Oronde Gadsden before a game, 2001.

1. The various shots and angles from a television broadcast are used for instant replay review by NFL game officials. **2.** An NFL Films cameraman records the action of a game between the Pittsburgh Steelers and the Baltimore Ravens, 2002. **3.** Tampa Bay Buccaneers wide receiver Joe Jurevicius at a Super Bowl XXXVII press conference in San Diego. **4.** New York Jets running back Curtis Martin tracked by a video cameraman. **5.** Video cameraman on a crane high above the action, 2002.

Hundreds of journalists from around the world descend upon the members of the Tampa Bay Buccaneers on Media Day before Super Bowl XXXVII.

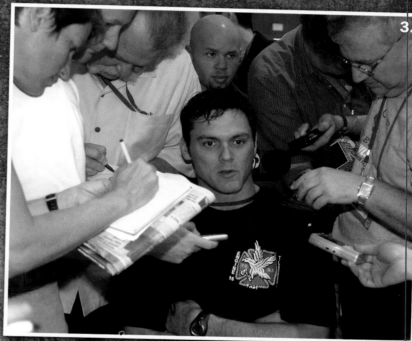

THE FANS

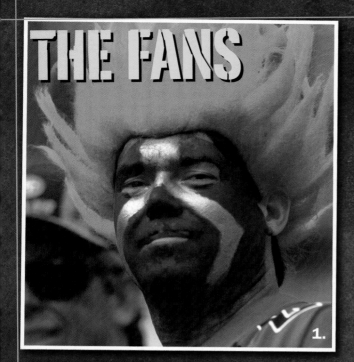

1.

2.

10.

11.

9.

8.

3.

4.

Enthusiastic Eagles fans in the upper deck at the Philadelphia Eagles' last home game at Veterans Stadium, 2002.

5.

7.

6.

Atlanta Falcons cheerleaders welcome star running back Jamal Anderson in pregame introductions at SB XXXIII in Miami.

Tampa Bay Buccaneers quarterback Brad Johnson fires the team up before a game, 2002.

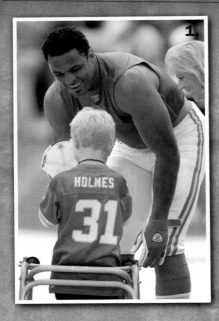

1. Tight end Tony Gonzalez of the Kansas City Chiefs signs an autograph for a child before a game, 2002. 2. Miami Dolphins wide receiver Cris Carter signs autographs at Pro Player Stadium in Miami, 2002. 3. Green Bay Packers players huddle at mid-field before a game in St. Louis, 2001 playoffs. 4. Defensive back Jarrod Cooper of the Carolina Panthers adjusts his pads prior to a game, 2002. 5. Opening ceremony before a Dallas Cowboys vs. San Diego Chargers game, 2001.

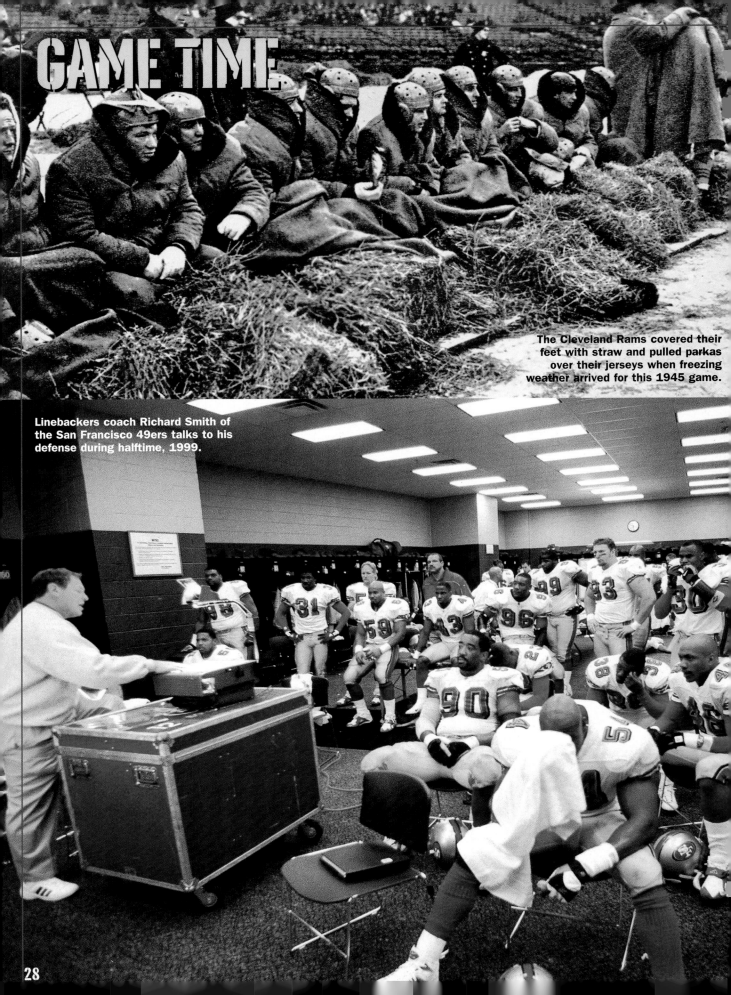

GAME TIME

The Cleveland Rams covered their feet with straw and pulled parkas over their jerseys when freezing weather arrived for this 1945 game.

Linebackers coach Richard Smith of the San Francisco 49ers talks to his defense during halftime, 1999.

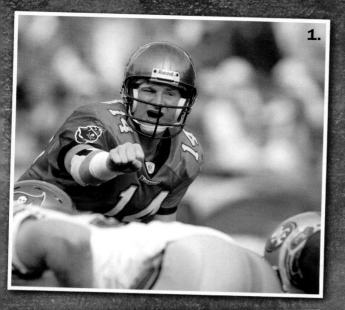

1.

2.

3.

4.

1. Tampa Bay Buccaneers quarterback Brad Johnson calls a play against the San Francisco 49ers. 2. Running back Ricky Watters of the Seattle Seahawks loses his helmet but holds on to the ball after getting hit by Zach Thomas and Kenny Mixon of the Miami Dolphins, 2000. 3. Green Bay Packers running back Dorsey Levens does the "Lambeau Leap" into the arms of Packers fans to celebrate a touchdown, 1998. 4. The mood on the Jacksonville Jaguars bench is solemn during the final moments of a tough loss for the team, 2001.

WINNING

Kicker Adam Venatieri is mobbed by his New England Patriots teammates after hitting the winning field goal in overtime in an epic playoff game versus the Oakland Raiders, 2002.

1. Excitement is in the air as St. Louis Rams fans salute their defending Super Bowl Champs at the 2000 season opener. 2. Tackle Barry Simms of the Oakland Raiders celebrates a teammate's touchdown with a spike, 2002. 3. Quarterback Brett Favre rejoices as the Packers score during a game, 1996. 4. Near the end of his Hall of Fame career, John Elway finally wins the big prize in 1998—Super Bowl XXXII.

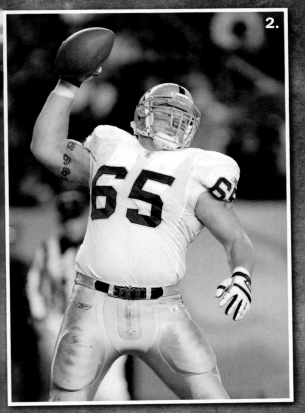

Tampa Bay Buccaneers teammates celebrate a touchdown during their Super Bowl XXXVII victory over the Oakland Raiders, 2003.